skin

Previous Walt McDonald First-Book Winners

Setting the World in Order, Rick Campbell
Heartwood, Miriam Vermilya
Into a Thousand Mouths, Janice Whittington
A Desk in the Elephant House, Cathryn Essinger
Stalking Joy, Margaret Benbow
An Animal of the Sixth Day, Laura Fargas
Anna and the Steel Mill, Deborah Burnham
The Andrew Poems, Shelly Wagner
Between Towns, Laurie Kutchins
The Love That Ended Yesterday in Texas, Cathy Smith Bowers

skin
april lindner

Texas Tech University Press

This book was set in Caslon 540 BT. The paper used in this book meets the minimum requirements of ANSI/NISO Z39.48-1992 (R1997).∞
Printed in the United States of America

Design by Brandi Price

Credits to the Epigraphs: (page viii) *Remembering the Bone House* by Nancy Mairs Copyright © 1989, 1995 by Nancy Mairs. Reprinted by permission of Beacon Press, Boston. "I." *Selected Poems* by Jorge Luis Borges, edited by Alexander Coleman, translated by Alastair Reid. (page 34) Obituary, *The Dallas Morning News*, 9 January 1965.

Library of Congress Cataloging-in-Publication Data
Lindner, April.
  Skin / April Lindner.
    p. cm. — (The Walt McDonald first-book poetry series)
  ISBN 0-89672-484-0 (cloth : alk. paper)
  I. Title. II. Series.
  PS3612.I55 S54 2002
  811'.6—dc21
                                        2001007153

        01 02 03 04 05 06 07 08 09 / 9 8 7 6 5 4 3 2 1

Texas Tech University Press
Box 41037
Lubbock, Texas 79409-1037 USA

1-800-832-4042

ttup@ttu.edu

www.ttup.ttu.edu

for andré

Acknowledgments

The author gratefully acknowledges the following journals, where these poems originally appeared, some in slightly different versions:

   Able Muse (an on-line poetry journal): "Girl."
   Birmingham Poetry Review: "Montauk" and "Beard"
   Cincinnati Poetry Review: "Learning to Float"
   Crazyhorse: "Hurricane"
   Farmer's Market: "5:25 on the I.R.T."
   The Formalist: "Crystal"
   The Greensboro Review:" Peep Show"
   The Louisville Review: "Ghosts"
   The Paris Review: "The Rubin Vase"
   Rhino: "What I Didn't Tell You"
   The Spoon River Quarterly: "Desks"

"Condom," "Inoculation," "A Brief Primer of Worries," and "Kokoschka's Doll," are reprinted from *Prairie Schooner* by permission of the University of Nebraska Press, copyright 1992 and 1995, the University of Nebraska Press. "Seascape" first appeared in the anthology *Stories From Where We Live: The North Atlantic Coast,* edited by Sara St. Antoine. Minneapolis: Milkweed Editions, 2000.

   In writing the poems on the life of Alma Mahler-Werfel, I relied heavily on several sources, including Susan Keegan's *The Bride of the Wind,* Karen Monson's *Alma Mahler: Muse to Genius;* Frank Whitford's *Oskar Kokoschka*; Henry-Louis de La Grange's *Mahler,* vol. 1; Alma's diaries (translated by Anthony Beaumont); and her memoir, *And the Bridge is Love,* written in collaboration with E. B. Ashton, whose full citations appear under Further Reading.

   Heartfelt thanks to those who nurtured these and earlier poems, including Andrew Hudgins, Don Bogen, John Drury, Maureen Fry, Dana Gioia, Thomas Lux, Cornelius Eady, Joan Larkin, Marilyn Nelson, Mekeel McBride, Charles Simic, Kate Knapp Johnson, and Nancy Kenworthy. Thanks to the Ohio Arts

Council and the University of Cincinnati's Taft Memorial and Elliston-Lanzit Funds for financial support. Finally, thanks to those who have provided emotional sustenance along the way, especially Grace, Edward, and Melody Lindner; Virginia Andros; Dorothee Heisenberg; Chris Norris Bamberger; Eric Drogin; and André, Eli, and Noah St. Amant.

Contents

vii Acknowledgments
xi Introduction

I

3 Inoculation
4 Desks
6 Peep Show
7 What I Wanted
8 Tornado Watch
9 Ghosts
10 Moving
11 Coffee Break
12 Spice
14 Supper
15 The Way We Touch Today
17 Midtown
18 5:25 on the I.R.T.
19 Seascape
20 Montauk
22 A Bestiary
23 Condom
24 Quickening
25 Ultrasound
26 A Brief Primer of Worries
28 Fontanel
29 Hurricane
30 A Lesson
31 Splinter
32 Milk Tooth

II

35 Alma Speaks of Childhood
36 The Kiss
38 Counterpoint
40 Letter from Gustav Mahler
41 Frau Mahler
46 Mahler's Death
47 Kokoschka
48 Cut Flowers
49 Alma at Eighty
50 Last Words

III

53 Daylight
54 What I Didn't Tell You
56 Girl
57 On Leafing Through a Catalogue of
       William Bailey's Paintings
58 Portrait in Negative Space
59 Erotomania
65 First Kiss
66 Kokoschka's Doll
69 Aversive Therapy
70 Learning to Float
72 Beard
73 Crystal
74 The Rubin Vase

Introduction

Haven't we all been told how beauty is thin as truth, and don't we believe and disbelieve this "lie we'd carve and starve for. / We'd suck it till the juice ran down our arms" ("Girl")? Skin compels us, repels us. Beauty may be only skin deep, a fine covering—sensuous, at times translucent, almost transparent, and yet so obdurate. Skin insulates, guarding its vital organs just beneath this surface that teases us to peek, to try to penetrate ("Ghosts"). We call this desire by many names, the best of which is *love*. April Lindner's sensuously orchestrated collection of poems conveys the beauty and truth of love, how we know it to be paradoxical, obsessive, fearful, rapacious, holy. Love poems like these strike our senses the "way an onion's scent / clings to . . . fingers," refusing "to be camouflaged / by hand cream or perfume" ("Erotomania"). We come to such poems "bringing / our rough fingertips and greedy eyes" ("On Leafing Through a Catalogue of William Bailey's Paintings")—"the hunger of skin for skin" ("Quickening").

In this collection, skin and its hunger figure both literally and metaphorically, revealing a woman's history of desire—what she sees, not necessarily what she gets. Aren't all brides beautiful? Don't all grooms promise to love, to protect? And when they run the gauntlet of rice and cheering friends from chapel to getaway car, can this couple believe they will soon be "absolved by . . . [their] . . . dull lives" ("Coffee Break")? Or will one of the lovers flee inland ("Hurricane"), leaving the other "snarled in dreams, the complicated kind" with an "epic cast of characters who flicker onscreen / to speak portentous words" ("Daylight")? Having promised to return, they don't. All too often, "the dream taste / fades" ("Daylight"), and skin begins "to slough off into dust, the daily tug / toward obsolescence" ("Girl").

Then again, why does living happily ever after mean the glass slipper never breaks; the prince never aches for the woman he refused ("Portrait in Negative Space"); the princess never conjures up a "blue-eyed stranger" to spin her "weightless / for a frozen moment in his arms" ("Tornado Warning")? Appearance and reality. Beauty and truth. Isn't it all in the seeing, the "inner eye" unable to "hold / two views at once"? The viewer could look away, glance back, and see "a different picture" ("The Rubin Vase").

The three sections of *Skin* offer complementary portraits of desire and fulfillment, the union of a woman and a man, separated only by the thinnest of skin. The poems in Section I permit us to see desire from the point of view of a young wife and mother as she considers the consequences of hunger, the touch of skin on skin. It is what she expected; it is not what she expected. It is the paradox of the smallpox inoculation: having been handed over to the good doctor with a needle, the child must experience pain to be immune from pain, then carry the scar of this immunity "big as a nickel, deep as the print / a thumb leaves in dough" ("Inoculation"). Opening the first section and the book's poetic sequence, "Inoculation" sets the tone of the collection and introduces its central, paradoxical, thematic motif: "My fingers want and don't want / to read the forgotten sting / in every stranger's skin." Everyone —lover, husband, wife, child—is a stranger, and the closest a woman and a man can come to union is still a chasm, "that thin film of air / between our skins" ("The Rubin Vase").

Section I moves quickly from the "extravagant" inattentiveness of ninth-grade girls at their desks, each basking "in her own heat, / flushed and gloriously dull as a tongue / after a salty first course" ("Desks") to the sensuous innocence of the young wife and her husband "[b]razen" in their "clean skins, so sure / what pleasure . . . [their] . . . bodies could give / must be good" ("Peep Show"). Although the young wife needs to bring order and control to beauty—"to trim each object into pretty shapes: / hedges squared, wildflowers tamed" ("What I Wanted"), she confesses in "Tornado Warning" that the love she feels for her husband is not as safe as he expects. There are days when a rangy, "blue-eyed stranger" could send her soaring, teetering "on the headlong edge of smash." A husband must take care not to believe his wife's "place in this kitchen / permanent as mortar" ("Ghosts"). The wife soon comes to know that beneath skin, each interior is "locked and off-limits, / like rooms we lived in houses ago" ("Moving"). "Spice" reveals the wife's almost desperate faith, saving "jars for the transparent hope / of what they'll hold." At supper, she imagines a stranger in the rain, the dark outside her lit window that must seem to him "both warm and cold, a kiss withheld" ("Supper").

Seemingly insulated from the world outside her marriage, she acknowledges in "The Way We Touch Today" her "low-grade, chronic longing / for voice and motion, the faint scent of skin," but she knows also that "seeing any face too close, its features / dissolving into moonscape, peaks and craters" transports the viewer from "the familiar into strange and back again."

Having established in these opening poems the motif of wanting and not wanting, of attraction and fear of attraction, of the marks in skin that identify us both to lovers and to strangers, the poems in the last half of Section I follow the young wife into the market place of "dull lives" ("Coffee Break")—midtown and the world of commerce, the "bare arms of strangers" rubbing on the subway as they "lurch / roughly in the same direction" ("5:25 on the I. R. T."). The wife and her husband thirst "for the ocean's pomp and flash" ("Montauk"), settling for "testing the resistance of each other's skin" ("Bestiary"). When the child is conceived, it seems a miracle of its parents' "fumblings, / only the hunger of skin for skin" ("Quickening"). They shiver and are "oddly gladdened" ("Condom"), especially the mother-to-be as she lays her hand on her belly to feel the child's pulse ("Quickening") and tacks to the walls ultrasound photos of *Your son* ("Ultrasound"). Then come birth and the mother's worries: Will she ever "learn" her child ("A Brief Primer of Worries")? Will her child know her by scent before he learns her name ("Fontanel")? Then the husband flees "after years of false alarms," and the child grows "tall enough / to take . . . [his mother's] . . . hand and venture into wind" ("Hurricane"). Faced "with so much ocean," he, unlike his anxious mother, can laugh at what lies before him ("Hurricane").

In "Splinter," the child, Eli, is five, and now his mother has taken on the role of the doctor in the first poem, "Inoculation." Now, it is she who must inflict pain to dig out the splinter in her child's thumb. She fears this splinter will "ride the bloodstream / straight to the heart," so she squeezes the boy's wrist and picks "at the flesh / that gives its enemy a home." She could "[r]elax and trust, or draw some blood." She is afraid for her son and chooses to play it safe, penetrating his skin for love's sake. "Milk Tooth," the last poem in Section I, concludes this opening view of desire and its consequences with the wife and mother acknowledging her participation in the union, skin on skin, that resulted in her son's handing over his milk tooth, "flat as the coin it will become" under his pillow. Now his mother can acknowledge this truth: "on the cusp between woman and girl / I let a man root out my wisdom / and was glad to give it away."

The middle section of *Skin* is a sequence of ten persona poems spoken by Alma Mahler Werfel, considered the most beautiful woman in Vienna at the turn of the twentieth-century. The poems permit Alma to speak first hand about desire and how it defines a woman. She details her love and admiration for her father and for her illustrious husbands and lovers. Alma seems both earth mother and femme fatale, both willing victim and seductive temptress. Her open life and loves provide the counterpoint to the young wife and mother of the first section and lead to the more experienced, more wary wife and lover of the third section.

From her first kiss at eighteen, Alma "a virgin of high birth," follows her own course of love. The man who kisses her is no hormone-driven teenager, but Klimt the artist—"middle-aged and syphilitic, / unsuitable" ("The Kiss"). In "Counterpoint," Alma explains how she "chose" Gustav Mahler, "a song to marry," and Alexander Zemlinsky, "a second song / to flow beneath . . . [the first] . . . like an undertow." Marrying Mahler, Alma knows, means she will have to be his wife, not his colleague ("Letter from Gustav Mahler"). Discounting her pregnancy and propriety, she wonders what compelled her to accept the proposal of a man whose music she doesn't like. She concludes that she married him for his "transfigured face, those parted lips" ("Frau Mahler"). This marriage teaches her the responsibilities and the grief of motherhood. She blames Mahler for the death of their child Putzi. She had feared Mahler's composing his famous *Kindertotenlieder* indifferent to irony and superstition. Alma asks, "What kind of father chooses such a poem / to set to music?" ("Frau Mahler"). She takes Walter Gropius for a lover. When Mahler dies, she takes Oskar Kokoschka, then marries Gropius. Later she marries Franz Werfel. She has to bear the grief of an abortion and a miscarriage. She says, "Of course I lived to baptize my son, / to bury him, to tell / the necessary lies. Someone must live" ("Cut Flowers"). At eighty, Alma seems amazed that two rooms now hold all of her life. There are no more husbands and lovers: geniuses "grew fewer every year" ("Alma at Eighty"). She keeps "champagne in stock for celebrations," never skimps on "pearls or pancake makeup, / and never once wore panties" ("Alma at Eighty"). In "Last Words," Alma sums up her life of desire and fulfillment: "It was given me to hold the reins / for the horsemen of light." Now, Death is her handsome lover. He needs her. Bred to be a lady, she became seductress, wife, and mother. Now she concludes, "If there was a cost, I have forgotten."

The persona of Section III is very much aware of the cost. She is no longer the young wife and mother of Section I. She is now more open about that part of her that is Alma Mahler Werfel. Now, in "Daylight," she can admit: "You bought the drama / wholesale, despite clues," despite "his touch / which should have tipped you off." Now she is "snarled in dreams," and these dreams are "the complicated kind." In this new light of day, she recognizes that love, beauty, truth are not black and white but "umpteen shades of silver." She has a new perspective. She has become, in "What I Didn't Tell You," "schooled in the ways / of the swallow," tracing "her own peculiar loops / against the sky". She admits her strength, her desire, how she "stole what . . . [she] . . . chose / from each" imagined lover—"every man . . . [she] . . . met," lying with each "to feel the bones / of . . . [her] . . . face change shape in his hands."

"Girl" reveals a wiser woman who no longer "glows and beckons" to every man, knowing each wants her. Now she knows "her flesh exhausted / by its own weight," and John Keats's "Beauty is truth, truth beauty—that is all" has become the "lie we'd carve and starve for." She feels "shipwrecked" by beauty's "ceaseless motion" and confesses that reaching for beauty's "prow," she only catches its "wake."

In "On Leafing Through a Catalogue of William Bailey's Paintings," the persona admits that the artist, the man, knows how to make us "see / deeper than we'd choose" when we look at his seductive "women, cool and grave." What the persona sees is what this man exposes about *woman*; the persona can understand why the viewer's eyes are "greedy" for this "pattern of shadows and luster, / a cluster of eggs displayed on a table, / a long, fallopian throat."

In the multiple-poem "Erotomania," the poet-persona assumes yet other personas to exposes the eroticism of the ordinary, how the grocer packing the paper bag with "bleeding strawberries, the dull ache of mushrooms," with "silken avocado," fills his customer's dreams with "flesh smooth as cream, green as willows" ("Diane G."). And for her physician, the persona of "Elizabeth M." opens her throat, says "*aaah*" as his "flashlight warms . . . [her] . . . tongue." She admits she "shouldn't say this," but once a year when she spreads herself "inside out" to "receive the speculum's sharp tongue," she knows she has come to allow her doctor's "gloved and gentle fingers" to prize her down to her "very cells." In answer to his question, she lies, says he is not hurting her.

In poem "3" of "Erotomania," the persona explains that "to love, we must go / a little mad" like Diane G. and Elizabeth M. and like the obsessed lover in "David R.," hunkered and waiting outside in the "square of light" cast by the woman's window. And the poet-persona speaking in her own voice in poem "6" of "Erotomania" confesses how desire has also made her "crazy, like those others." The man she married accepts her ragged sweats, her obtuse statements, her belching on the street; but what she admits is "sick" is that sometimes she feels "homesick" for the man whose approval she starved for—turning back flips, dyeing her hair because her lover was "*hot for blondes*," "sailing through," her hair unsinged, the lion tamer's "burning hoops."

In "Kokoschka's Doll," the persona continues the motif of desire running "amuck," driving a man, a woman, insane and self-destructive as they slip from their clothes to try to bring their lovers ease and release. Sometimes lovers are "stony as the lions on library steps"; sometimes they are reckless as their dreams, "simpler to embrace than life."

"Aversive Therapy" reveals the persona's struggle to banish her lover, to "stop / loving you." To do this, she must torment herself by conjuring up her lover's indiscretions—memories that scorched her throat with bile, spurred her pulse—"memories of the summer / . . . [he] . . . banged bones with a lifeguard while . . . [the persona] . . . waited / for a phone call, a postcard." Though she is successful with this means of therapy, the persona admits her jealousy was really for her lover's lover, "that girl who knew exactly what she loved."

The persona's examination of the beauty and truth of desire has led to a kind of reconciliation, a compromise, an acknowledgment of the precarious nature of love. Now she accepts that love is like learning to float—the woman "moored" by the man's hand, trusting "he won't let go" ("Learning to Float"). She acknowledges the impossibility of knowing a man. It is a "sinuous path / from chin to soles" ("Beard"). The more she stares at her lover, the more his "edges blur" until his name "dissolves to babble"—*husband, lover, brother, father, stranger*" ("Beard"). And even though in the final poem, "The Rubin Vase," she can say, "As if our skins were porous and your soul / were liquid, you poured into me" ("Crystal"), she is still very much aware of that "space between / two people," that "thin film of air / between our skins." And she still wants and doesn't want the object of her desire: "One day I can't / abide your touch, the next day I can't stand / its absence." What she has come to know at this point in her history of desire is that desire between a woman and a man is both blessing and curse, precarious as the "chasm" formed by the man's body lowering "to press against . . . [the woman's] . . . upward-arching body." They are both aware of the chasm; they know that "once seen," it can't "be overlooked." More importantly, for desire, for a relationship, to endure, the chasm *must not* be overlooked.

Robert Fink
Abilene, Texas, 2002

Fortunately, one simply cannot *be* without being a body.
One simply *is* inches of supple skin and foot after foot of gut,
slosh of blood, thud of heart, lick of tongue, brain humped
and folded into skull. And it is as a body that one inhabits the
past and it inhabits one's body.

Nancy Mairs
Remembering the Bone House

The skull within, the secret, shuttered heart,
the byways of the blood I never see
the underworld of dreaming, that Proteus,
the nape, the viscera, the skeleton.
I am all those things.

Jorge Luis Borges
(tr. Alastair Reid)
"I"

Inoculation

Etched high on the back of your arm,
as big as a nickel, deep as the print
a thumb leaves in dough, this saucer embraces
a flock of deeper pocks. On sleeveless days
we see how some scars fade, like the full moon
after sunrise, while some, decades old,
persist as clearly as the day the doctor
stamped them there, pain clanging in the arm
like a dropped kettle, echoing down
to the stricken fingertips—how deep
the needles must have gone to leave such dents.
My fingers want and don't want
to read the forgotten sting
in every stranger's skin, the way I don't dare trace
the seam above your eyebrow from that day
you tripped and hit the corner of a brick.
Tender red snake, badly matched patch,
it shows how hard the body tries
to hide its healing. I almost believe
what's engraved there, how there's nothing
our cells can't assemble, worker ants,
the bread divided, trundled down the hole
the crumbs piled high, a makeshift loaf.
The ghost of your vaccine is a mirage,
the skin as taut as ice. The puncture holes
have closed through which they fed you
chicken pox and rubeola, just enough
to make your white blood cells gang up,
little vigilantes, but the brand
still advertises what we would forget—
the child bribed with candy, handed over,
disbelieving the needle even as his arm
bruises in the doctor's ample hand.

Desks

The ninth grade trickles daily through this room.
Faces half-lit by the bank of broad windows,
they gaze unseeing at the streamlined cross
nailed above the board. Their blue serge uniforms
can't hide the quirks they despise
and flaunt: Jessica's hair
more magenta than red; Nikki's spiky bangs
and candied lips; Lauren's freckled legs.
Class over, they orbit each other
as though gravity already has settled
who will be Jupiter, who will be its moons,
each girl propelled by some nameless torque
that leads her to the same place every day,
which may be why one seat in back attracts
only reckless girls who flail their hands
at every question, who would never,
right or wrong, be overlooked. Like generals at the head,
the straight-A's fidget in their ironed blouses,
faces framed by metal barrettes, while the deep
anonymous middle is refuge to quiet C's,
eyes down, attendant to the balance beam
they tread, on one side the pitfall of saying
something dumb, on the still-worse other hand,
being sucked up into smartness, into caring
too much. And those who drift to the fringes,
choosing window seats as if for quick escape,
sit loosely stitched in place, heavy headed
and fertile as sunflowers. Their inattention
is extravagant; each basks in her own heat,
flushed and gloriously dull as a tongue

after a salty first course. How can books
say anything to her when each crisp page
drinks moisture from her fingertips and wilts?
Smugly she waits for her classmates
to join her in the doorless corridor
she inhabits, helplessly enthralled
by its baroque scrolls, its merciless curvature,
every mirror reporting fresh distortions.

Peep Show

Tonight we forget again to draw the shade,
pass from room to room, backlit like paper dolls
in a diorama. At bedtime, I remember the window,

single unblinking eye, and must count back
the hours. What striptease did we dance tonight?
Brazen in our clean skins, so sure

what pleasure our bodies could give
must be good. Did someone catch you
washing dishes, nude in the hot spray?

Or me, slipping out of my blouse,
the spotted bulb casting dappled light
along my back? Surely no stranger waits

in that dark patch between streetlamps
for just such luck. From here I can watch
the boys across the way, in striped pajamas,

belly down before the television, each head
haloed in red, then blue, then green.
When we were new here, you hurried home

one night in the dark and a man you didn't know
stepped in your path, jaw first, to hiss:
Hey mister, that girl you live with,

is she good? And for months
I scanned the empty street and wondered, for weeks
I appraised my flesh in the mirror, nipples

sharp, belly soft as a scoop of vanilla,
hating the nerve endings that sprang awake,
glad as harem girls at the merest touch.

What I Wanted

The pear tree I wanted
for its blossoms, its abundance,
bears long-necked odalisques in flimsy coats,
too hard all summer and then too soft,
a pulp that summons wasps.
Nothing's left to arrange in a blue-glazed bowl.

The morning glories we planted
for their tender faces, their genteel leaves,
lasso sunward up fence posts, scale the swing set,
their tendrils rising overnight
to bind and strangle every upright thing
in this square plot. Mowed down,
their numbers double. I can't change

the morning glories, the pear tree;
can't banish the wasps, or learn to like
their dartlike bodies zeroing in,
their hunger so much simpler than my need
to trim each object into pretty shapes:
hedges squared, wildflowers tamed,
roses trained to the trellis,
and stripped of thorn.

Tornado Watch

When skies engorged with rain
bruise indigo and lightning
sizzles like hot fat, when sheets
of struck tin draw in close,
we tune our radio for updates. In Ohio,
any thunderhead might roll into a funnel
and skip across hilltops or lumber through
to flatten red brick ranches. It's wise
to stay indoors and grumble gently
at lawn work left undone, to listen
for the siren cranking to a howl,
gooseflesh rising in slow motion
as we carry our sons to the cellar.
Do you know how I long
for that whistle, for God's magnet
to summon each nail till our clapboards scatter?
With care we've hung curtains, staked tomatoes,
painted the walls cinnamon and cream
with the smallest brush, getting each edge
so straight only I know
where the colors bleed and blur.
These rooms are spun of hours and days,
of the years it took to stumble into you
and reach those mutual conclusions
called *love*, to draw that blueprint,
marriage. Still, my pulse bubbles
each time a twister glances past,
rangy as a blue-eyed stranger.
How little it would take to spin me weightless
for a frozen moment in his arms
brisk and capricious, how little to soar
and teeter on the headlong edge of smash.

Ghosts

Whites going yellow, periwinkles
beginning to dim, the wallpaper
curls its invitation
to peek under skin at vital organs.
Where plaster should be, I find
space, and crumbling mortar, rafters
naked as a ribcage, the paper
glued to air, a trick played on posterity.
I've heard of old houses like this one,
with ghosts who chill the rooms as they pass,
floorboards rejoicing, women who weep
in nurseries, little girls in pinafores
who scatter book reports and rattle silverware.
But in this house of scrubbed cupboards
and incandescent bulbs, the only ghosts
are scars on doorframes, layers of paint
that tell time's passage like tree rings,
and those marks made to say
I live here and will always. A stranger chose
the tiles in this mosaic countertop—
a scorpion, a cow, shards of a teacup—
believing her place in this kitchen
permanent as mortar. Sometimes at night
I slip out to the deck to lie on my back
and imagine the constellations are,
by air rights, mine. Moving in, we found
confetti in the corners, tiny Mylar
stars and moons, and the pink dogwood
she planted, its adolescent trunk,
its blossoms scattered, festive, in the grass.

Moving

We shroud plates in newsprint,
bundle the kettle that sat on the stove
when we moved in. As proof
we lived here once, we'll leave
an onion's shed skin,
one coiled hair in a drain,
the spectral mask a dog's breath
imprinted on the window.

In different rooms,
we'll wipe ink from every platter,
scrub the kettle, find a spot
for albums fat with snapshots,
street maps of cities we'd like to revisit.

Last, we'll pierce the wall
to hang the faces we call ours:
bride face, groom face, infant face,
their interiors locked and off-limits,
like rooms we lived in, houses ago.

Coffee Break

A still procession of bodies,
naked, slender, single file,
heads stripped of hair, weaves through a room
in the building next door, lingers
in bruise-colored light.

We see for the first time
that room, those bodies
obscured by smudges and dust. I want

to bend back over my work.
Not to have seen. I want for you
not to have witnessed my seeing.
But I am trapped in your eyes
like a dragonfly in amber.

Then we remember, simply, where we are.
We see workmen on the fire escape
Joking, unwrapping sandwiches.

Sure enough, each wraith
is armless, white skin blank
of breasts or sex, all those faces
split by the same grim grin.

A manikin factory. We can turn back
to these black machines, our separate reams
of onionskin; we can believe ourselves
absolved by our dull lives.

Spice

I save jars for the transparent hope
of what they'll hold, and later I save
what's in those jars past pungency,

lug them from one city to the next.
My pantry's bottom shelf recalls
an Indian grocery, bolts of silvered cloth,

sitar on eight-track tapes. The homesick owner
fussed over his only Anglo customer,
guiding me through the dusty shelves out back

past lentils, yellow, pink, and black,
past burlap sacks of *basmati,* to the spices
whose names I loved, whose perfumes I had to own:

garam masala, amchoor, fenugreek,
even *asafetida,* the fetid root
whose musk seeps through mason glass

to fog the air with gold. Saffron filaments,
cardamom pods, black and green.
Here's a souvenir mailed from Barbados,

nutmegs ground to slivers, impossible
to grate without shredding finger skin,
and from an Asian market in Toledo

this powder I bought for its pretty bottle
and licked from my palm on the drive home—
orange peel? red pepper? poppy seed?—

conjuring cool tatami floors, rice paper,
a tea ceremony's slow unfolding. Now I linger
at this small glass skyline in the shadows,

this shrine to continents I planned to reach
and haven't yet, my fingertips burnished,
the air a billowing veil of coriander.

Supper

Turn the knob. The burner ticks
then exhales flame in a swift up burst,
its dim roar like the surf. Your kitchen burns white,
lamplight on enamel, warm with the promise
of bread and soup. Outside the night rains ink.
To a stranger bracing his umbrella,
think how your lit window must seem
both warm and cold, a kiss withheld,
lights strung above a distant patio.
Think how your bare arm, glimpsed
as you chop celery or grate a carrot
glows like one link in a necklace.
How the clink of silverware on porcelain
carries to the street. As you unfold your napkin,
book spread beside your plate, consider
the ticking of rain against pavement,
the stoplight red and steady as a flame.

The Way We Touch Today

You are one phone call, one e-mail away,
and so the way I miss you is irrational—
not unlike my low-grade, chronic longing
for voice and motion, the faint scent of skin.
Instead I pass the evening in this room,
sealed off from wind and rain by glass and plaster.
I dawdle at the screen, drink its glib promises
(engines that search the air, trawl in the lost)
I spell your name out, fingers on each key
brisk as a shoulder tap, and in the corner,
a globe spins, clouds unfurl, and some slick gizmo
spins through a list of names and spits up yours—
a rare, half-funny name just letters off
from dragon, or your high school hobby, druggin'.
The cursor, my small stand in, bathes your name
in light pale as the moon, cool as the sliver
that shines beneath my door, signals me here.
I feel my pulse jump as I drag you in,
and when I do, am startled by a face
I'd half forgotten, theme with variation.
This is your younger brother, and his posture
—formal at a table set with silver,
his slender torso braced by arms like yours
as if for strong wind, bad news, or more likely,
for powerful amusement, both hands cupping
the table corners—this stance is pure you.
His shirt is blue, his beard recently trimmed.
Someone who loved him set him here, a tribute
more mutable than stone, and if
I want to I can click to see *his* face,
to monkey up the ladder of abstraction

masked as relationship. My distant friend,
remember how you typed the news, hit "enter"?:
I'm flying home. My brother killed himself . . .
your words made doubly still by their translation
into blue pixels gathered on white ground.
To see your brother from this triple distance—
two hundred miles, two years, and death—is oddly
like seeing any face too close, its features
dissolving into moonscape, peaks and craters,
familiar into strange and back again.
I press my fingertips to humming glass.

For Eric

Midtown

Shouldering forward in a charcoal coat,
I'd keep alert for manholes, sidewalk cracks,
and blinking *don't walk* signs. I rarely paused
to note how the cathedral's vaulted windows
brood in blues and roses, dimmer from without,
the stone crevices inlaid with velvet soot,
or how the plain glass windows of the Bauhaus
line up like cemetery plots. It was a job,
ignoring the sky and the stream of faces
because a straight-on look would mean
I'd been seen back, been caught breaking the pact.
I paused for stoplights, traffic spinning past,
and if I dared look up, the buildings on all sides
shot skyward till not swooning meant resisting
the backward tug at my shoulders and calves,
the urge to drop down flat, the sky a blade
against my naked throat. Three years I trudged
and trudged, and loved the vertigo,
loved the skyscraper growing in my spine
as long as I didn't stop to divide
how many bridges by how many cars
the highways clogged with them, the air dark
with their dry breath. Until I thought too hard
about how there was no way out
but down, through the subway's parched throat.
Once I shot through an elevator's veins
to overlook the rainy patchwork blocks,
the stoplights beating red and green, the rivers
unpassable as moats at my right and my left,
merging at the island's tip, the icy sea
flat as glass. On my face, I felt
the lacerating wind, its faint burnt chestnut scent.
And in my ears the roar that seeps from midtown:
shouts and footsteps, horns and subway brakes,
muffled by distance, by each other,
a thousand voices canceled out to dust.

5:25 on the I.R.T.

The bare arms of strangers
rub on the subway as we lurch
roughly in the same direction,
two rows facing off,
minding the unspoken rules
that govern commuters. Voices grow
familiar in their strangeness,
each unraveling the strand
of this particular day while I pretend
to be listening to my skull's white noise.
There are times for raised glances to clink:
the power failure; the rush-hour suicide;
the man in good shoes who passes,
inexplicably, out; the brown-haired girl
who squeezes through strangers
to loosen his tie. But nobody's pain
calls her forth from this crowd of witnesses.
No tears give her permission.
I regard the dull green floor,
its pattern like tea leaves
waiting to be read.

Seascape

At low tide you can wade the cove
from Revere to Nahant, the warmed Atlantic
licking your knees, clouds of red algae
clinging to your calves. Along the damp
and wrinkled sand, sea worms curl
into pale rosettes, so many
they're difficult to miss. Keep leaning
against the current, trying to forget
the boulders worried down to rocks,
to pebbles, to the silt that wants
to suck you under. Let your feet
brush bottle tops and gutted clams
diminishing in the alchemy
of salt. A few miles out
a garbage scow shuttles its load,
dusky and slow as a seafaring mountain
against the bright sky. Keep north,
pocking the mud with temporary footprints
past gray-capped birds, half-breeds
of pigeon and gull, each one
declaring a small kingdom
with a stretch of pterodactyl wings.

Montauk

This beach is a reproach,
flush with what the sea rakes in,
plastic bags limp as jellyfish,
here a diaper, there a lost red pail.
All winter we thirsted
for the ocean's pomp and flash,

not this expanse of towels unfurled like flags,
men and women stretched and staking claim,
bodies ritually bared and glossed.
We dreamed an isolated rock
bleached by the Aegean, a fire
for roasting shellfish, our salted backs

cooling against white stone.
So now we keep struggling across sand
for that one slice of landscape
that hasn't been mapped out,
our own desert island to populate.
The sun broadcasts its invitation

through our suits, summer afternoon
invading our veins till we're even more aware
of all these strangers, teased as we are
with need. This sticky paradise of flesh
and junk the sea keeps washing back

mocks our desire. What upholstered this sand,
the urge to eat the meat and cast
the bones aside, the drive

to pass our genes along, mundane
because it isn't ours alone? Offshore,

cormorants list from a crag,
avid undertakers squinting for a glint of fish.
And just beneath this dark lace
of bubbles in damp sand, clams gulp
through parted lips of stone.

A Bestiary

Through our faulty screens they squeeze,
uninvited guests, these first
honeymoon weeks: ladybugs,
blue-headed flies, a raspy
parade of wasps, and one preying mantis
with his prehistoric stare.
A squirrel scratches at the window,

and a renegade jay
mistakes us for paradise, dive bombs the screen
with walnut skull, stubborn beak;
bounces off and tries again.
Some are sneakier: the gray identical

mouse brigades that nest
beneath the sink. And roaches,
a brown, scurrying few,
copulate in shadows under the toaster.

Their whiskers and antennae
quiver in our direction,
homing in. Sometimes I feel
their sharp eyes poking holes
in the dark where we lie

testing the resistance of each other's skin.
On nights like these, I hear
what might have been there always:
each cell of my body,
separate and planetary,
humming its own mutinous tune.

Condom

With a soundless rip
the pale balloon rends,
and what we perceive as a breakthrough
in our shared love, a tender flood
of trust, as if we could peel back
our skins and give each other
the stripped bouquet of nerves,
this crowning rush of selflessness, is born
of self. It's you I feel for once.
How smoothly the body seduces the mind.
The roots of joy flourish
in our membranes and bellies; much as I crave
your insight, what matters
is how you feed me buckwheat pancakes
with raspberry syrup, how you brush my hair
so hard the bristles
knead my scalp. Some would even say
the love of poetry is nothing
but the coursing of hormones
to the cerebrum. We shiver,
but are oddly gladdened by the sight
of shredded latex, by the steep ascent,
the imagined embrace; we can almost feel
a silken bean sprout, sightless, sexless,
blanketed by plush, lending weight
to my every breath. Oh happy relapse
like the last bright lungful of deliverance
the drowning are said to inhale, this giving in;
what relief it must be to even
the strongest swimmer, the undertow firm
as a parent, trustworthy, kind.

Quickening

At sunset, the lake's taut surface
begins, one peck at a time, to boil
with the mouths of feeding trout.
That's how it feels when I lie and wait
in stillness, for your pulse
just under my hand. This fizz
of surfacing bubbles is different
from the kicks you volunteer
when I expect them least,
motion from slumber, burst
of popcorn from a kernel.
Yesterday, like all the days before it,
nothing. Then one nudge,
and now this knocking, knocking.
Soon your white-lashed lids
will open, floodgates
letting the world swim in.
I can't say how we conjured you
with only our fumblings,
only the hunger of skin for skin.

Ultrasound

A gathering of pixels
wavers and shifts,
irresolute as clouds.
We can orbit this entire
briny planet, can see,
if not the heart itself
its storm systems,
a typhoon of blood
furling in and receding,
and in the skull's nimbus
a whorl, eye-shaped but blind,
like the single eye
on the Monarch's wing.
We can measure the spine,
hover above the head,
swoop to the foot soles,
peer up through the arc
of pelvis and thighbones
to find a delicate *fleur-de-lis*.
The technician can snap a switch,
deliver a picture into our hands,
white ink on black. *Your son*.
Tacked to the walls,
a nebula of faces floats
just beyond our reach.

A Brief Primer of Worries

My first despair: of ever
learning you, you slept so long
and deeply, those fingers
with their delicate, sharp nails

beyond your control and mine,
wandering your face, lacing it
with sparrow tracks. My next despair:
that anyone could see

from your troubled forehead
how already I'd failed you,
the web of first hair
clinging to your fists, the ruby stump

of your penis in its coat of curd,
struggling back from the operation
I'd ordered. And so many ways,
yet undreamed, to harm you still:

neck soft as an oyster,
the visible dark pulsing of blood
just under your skull's thin sheath.
Seized into being.

How could I name you mine?
Even as I nursed you, I'd despair.
Already you so plainly
were your own, eyes shut

against daylight, lamplight, my face,
as you sucked hunger away,
mustering yourself against the world.
All night my sleep wove

fitfully around yours,
till morning when the chimes
of subway cars washed in.
Half welcome, the sun

gave birth to our shadows,
and, drunk with milk, you rolled
still deeper into the refuge
of dreams. I didn't know

beneath those twitching lids,
those twin blue petals, already
the smoked glass was lightening
to drink me in.

for Eli

Fontanel

Here's the ravine, a stretch of skin
spanning the breach like a footbridge.
Canvas-thin, it trembles with the blood
that runs beneath. Something less tangible
courses there too, a whitewater flume
of images: the stretching housecat;
car keys that sing and catch light;
floorboards knotted with dark, animal eyes;
the window with its shifting square of sky.
All things equal, each thing startling,
and everything unmediated by the mind's
habitual grapple with *why*
and *so what*. You frown at a faded
wallpaper pineapple, and the membrane
flutters harder. I'm careful
when I comb your sparse brown hair.
When I sing your name I borrow a lilt
I'd never use in speech. The words
don't matter; I'm saying drink me while you can,
like milk. Let me be flesh and flannel,
hands that loosen your tangled blanket.
Know me by scent before you learn my name,
before doorknobs turn into doorknobs,
before the gates knit shut.

For Noah

Hurricane

In a season of wild forecasts, a real hurricane
at last lumbers in, all horizontal rain,
and Mixmaster wind. The town has fled inland

as you did after years of false alarms.
I hardly miss you anymore except
when blown salt seals the windows,

the roof groans, and the lights
blink off. When megaphone voices
cackle warnings from the boardwalk,

when waves vault the seawall, and a few
bold souls in wetsuits bob like gulls,
braving the heady swells for pleasure.

At high tide the ocean musters strength,
shoulders across the road to consider
our welcome mat and clapboards,

and relents. I hardly miss you.
Our son is tall enough
to take my hand and venture into wind,

to pick along the corrugated pipes
unearthed by storm and scattered
like the felled pillars of Rome.

He runs to gather every stone
the sea washed in, to cast it back,
to tease the surge, then dart

just past its reach, to perch
at the continent's edge and,
faced with so much ocean, laugh.

A Lesson

Imagining themselves concealed by dusk,
the children on my block part bushes
to look for black-striped snails.
They pick at the shells,
prod the damp meat with twigs,
or stomp for the crunch,
the starburst of shards.
Each has been taught
not to bite the breast, not to hit,
not to tear the fur from pets,
but by now each kid's been smacked
at least once by a bigger kid
who got away with it. Each has felt
a parent's offhand slap, or stood,
face upturned, in a cold rain of words.
Each has weighed his parents' *be gentle*s.
The children study moth blood—
red and wet, or black and sticky?—
roll shrieking through uncut grass
while nightfall lures out lightning bugs
whose bulbs when crushed
release a potent, cedary perfume.

Splinter

While I worry with a needle
his thumb's plump root stitched twice
by a sliver, Eli's eyes squeeze shut.
This can't hurt, but he flinches,
five years old and straining
for control. Tries not to. Flinches.
Once a friend held my hand
like this, palm up at a party,
traced my lifeline to dead end.
I laughed, but it's not disbelief
that keeps me from reading Eli's palm.
At my throat, a silver cross rubs
against *il corno*, and when I think
no one's looking, I cross myself,
knock wood. Our doctor claims
shards float below the skin in sacs
the body spins, but everyone knows
splinters ride the bloodstream
straight to the heart. What's worse?
Relax and trust, or draw some blood
and root the black thread out?
Better safe. I squeeze Eli's wrist,
and pick at the flesh
that gives its enemy a home.

Milk Tooth

Blood at the root. You hand it over
flat as the coin it will become
under your pillow. Little weight of bone,
its pale enamel bears a hint of shadow.
As a tool it's stone-aged, obsolete.
On your lower jaw a new dark door
leads to the cave under a tongue
moored by one thin thread. You let my finger
trespass at the gum where a knife
waits against silk. In dreams
my own bicuspids crumble like chalk
to say I was too greedy for the future,
to say I squandered time. It's true,
some nights I couldn't wait
for you to fall asleep. True, I rejoiced
when you could walk, my unencumbered arms
light as balloons. And yes, it's true:
on the cusp between woman and girl
I let a man root out my wisdom
and was glad to give it away.

II

Counterpoint
Poems on the Life of Alma Mahler Werfel

"Mrs. Alma Mahler Werfel, 85, 'the most beautiful woman in Vienna' at the turn of the century and the widow of composer Gustav Mahler, died yesterday at her home. . . . Mrs. Werfel, who was born Alma Schindler, daughter of the Austrian landscape painter Emile J. Schindler, also was married to Walter Gropius the architect, and to Franz Werfel the writer and poet . . . Mahler died in 1911 and his widow said she chose the expressionist painter, Oskar Kokoschka, as the next 'feather for her nest.'"

New York Telegram,
12 December 1964

"'All were geniuses, geniuses,' once rhapsodized Alma Werfel about her official husbands. . . . By her own statement, her loves included Oskar Kokoschka, the painter; Gerhart Hauptmann, the dramatist; Paul Kammerer, the biologist, and Ossip Gabrilowitsch, the pianist, conductor, and later husband of Clara Clemens . . . daughter of Mark Twain. . . . The late Mrs. Werfel was a monument to extraordinary facts of life. One was the puissance of romantic love, even in this century. Another was the basic utility of romantic love in the sublimations of artistic expression. Another was, of course, that womanhood itself is a primordial career."

The Dallas Morning News,
9 January 1965

"To be like him—my only wish.
I have two souls: I know it."

Alma Schindler, age 22

Alma Speaks of Childhood

In his studio I'd practice keeping still
for a chance to breathe turpentine
and linseed oil, to watch his hand
propel the brush. When I was eight,
he read me *Faust* until I wept
and Mother seized the book.
With cracks in his only shoes
he hired a cab for a month
to save his soles. Somehow
he found us a castle to live in,
its onion turret clearing the lindens.
A nervous child, I cherished one dream:
an olive grove, a row of studios,
where geniuses could live
for art alone, and for myself
a gondola, velvet draperies
trailing astern. When Papa died,
Mother locked us up, but I escaped
to find him in his wooden box,
pale and noble as a marble god.
At my piano I sang Wagner
till my voice dwindled
to a rasp. How else to forget
his gold-embroidered pall,
Mama at the funeral
crying too noisily. She married,
poor woman, when I was eighteen—
a pupil of Papa's, his profile coarse
as a medieval carving of St. Joseph.
Who would take the pendulum, I wondered,
when she's already had the whole clock?

The Kiss

When he seized me abruptly
in Genoa, Klimt hadn't yet
layered his women with gold.
This was before Danae's
ice-mottled thigh, the honed nipples
of Judith, before *Fulfillment*,

the rapt lovers awash
in gale-spun waves. I was eighteen,
a virgin of high birth, and Klimt,
middle-aged and syphilitic,
unsuitable. So we loved

as we could, that Italian holiday,
Mama studying my diary,
trailing me everywhere. I remember
our kiss not as it must have been—
the searing sun, the crowds of tourists—
but as *The Kiss*. Some other girl,

her torso broken by red
and violet islands, lets gravity
persuade her toward the steep
wildflower bed, the whole wise world
blurring to a charged abstraction.
My stepfather put Klimt on a train

back to Vienna, read me his letter:
*Forgive me, dear Sir, if I caused
anxiety. Fraulein Alma, I don't think*

she will find it hard to forget.
Later he painted a virgin wreathed
by her handmaidens' pearl pink flesh,

her bare white arms outstretched,
her body hidden by a sheet
or shroud. Swirls race across it,
a frenzy of pigment, teasing the eye:
She is not yours to know.

Counterpoint

From Vienna's best I chose Zemlinsky.
Most found him stunted, chinless,
the coffeehouse odor clinging

to his coat, but talent
lent him cachet, and we shared a taste
for Wagner. Over sheet music, our bowed heads

would all but touch as he played *Tristan*
while I strained my voice. One theme should dominate,
should set the mood, but when I wrote,

the melodies snared in their rush to be set down.
He called my songs chocolate, candied fruit,
white dress at dinner, said I needed

failure to teach me kindness; then I would write
as a woman. Still, under his hands,
my music grew deeper, more textured.

We met alone in a friend's Turkish parlor,
but my mother's *no* on my lips became my *no*.
How to choose among many tangled melodies

the one to dominate and set the mood?
And at a party, introduced to Mahler,
should I have minded his sharp gaze,

his tense frame poised to overhear
my conversation? He asked to see my songs.
Alexander Zemlinsky. Gustav Mahler.

One would be greater; my task was to guess
which man, but this meant casting off
a self, a set of possibilities.

Not easy for a girl who couldn't choose
a song to marry and a second song
to flow beneath it like an undertow.

Letter from Gustav Mahler

My dearest Almschi, those men who hover,
who flatter you, exchange big-sounding
words with you, they mistake the shell

for the nut. Everything in you
is yet unformed, unspoken.
Although you're infinitely adorable,

enchanting, with an upright soul,
richly talented, frank and self-assured,
you're still no personality,

but you could become the most sublime
object of my life, my stronghold,
in a word, my wife.

My Alma, look! In that little head
I love so indescribably dearly,
an obsession is fixed: your music.

But how do you picture the marriage
of two composers? How degrading
such competition would become.

Don't misunderstand, I wouldn't
regard you as plaything and housekeeper.
Still, you must become what I need:

my wife, not my colleague.
Your one profession, to make me happy.
I'm asking a great deal, a very great deal,

and, Alma, I must have your answer
before I see you on Saturday.
I'll send a servant to pick it up.

Frau Mahler

1

Why did I say yes? I wondered
even as I wrote the words, and pondered still
the morning Mahler arrived, beaming

beneath a cloudless sky. He was in debt,
and no beauty. As for his music,
what little I knew of it

I didn't like. Was it my mother's warnings,
my stepfather's protestations?
We made our vows in early March,

the church all but empty, hard rain
battering the roof. I was expecting,
but that wasn't the reason;

I'd already made up my mind.
As a lover, he'd proved distant,
burdened by my innocence,

tormented by his past affairs
with older women, his greater experience
which didn't, frankly, amount to much.

The press had revealed our engagement.
Gossips turned up everywhere I went
to watch me watch my fiancé conduct

his Fourth Symphony, new and strange
with beauties I hadn't yet divined.
Observed, I observed Gustav's profile,

his slight form swept by waves of music,
his arms outstretched before the Philharmonic,
that transfigured face, those parted lips.

2

After Gustav rang for the midwife
he tried to distract me
from the twisting knives
by seating me at his desk
and reading Kant.

Anna—our Gucki—tore through
at noon, and I awoke
to a stag beetle
dangling above my face.

I caught it for you, Mahler exulted
because you're so fond of animals.

3

Firmly taken by the arm and led away
from myself. That's how I felt.
While Gustav hummed, beat time

with his pencil, I would walk
aimlessly across the lawn,
lingering beneath the shifting lindens.

Sometimes I would try to sit
at my piano, fingers restless
with the memory of counterpoint,

to find my eyes had all but forgotten
that scattered, black language.

4

In this grim and howling storm,
I'd never have let the children outside . . .
Now these are but idle reflections.

What kind of father chooses such a poem
to set to music? Even as he wrote
his *Kindertotenlieder,* Gustav could hear
squeals from the garden, Putzi and Gucki
staining their pinafores, rolling in grass.

I'm not claiming my husband
didn't love our daughters, wasn't proud.
When Putzi was born breach, he roared,
That's my child! Show the world
the part it deserves. But he tempted fate

with songs about dead children.
When fever slowly stilled our Putzi's lungs,
he took to hiding in his room. The sky was red.
I scrubbed our largest table for the doctor,
tied back the dense curls and wept

till ordered outside. Servants stood guard
at Gustav's door to calm him should he wake
to the noise, the laryngotomy. I ran
along the lake shore, my screams
swallowed by the night, by rain.

Our Putzi suffered only one day more.
What kind of father? Warmhearted and frail
and deaf to the echoes of his careless words.

5

When away he wrote me daily letters
detailing his love, but in my presence
wouldn't listen. *So your budding dreams*

go unfulfilled, that's completely
up to you. My music, my thoughts,
these were nothing.

It wasn't the money,
though I wore the same dress for six years
and had no hat. It wasn't Putzi's death,

too much Benedictine, too many parties.
I needed something to spend my days on,
a change of air. At Tobelbad,

I bathed in hot springs, took a diet
of lettuce and buttermilk.
The doctor prescribed dancing,

and Walter Gropius was willing,
straight-backed and slender,
his moustache glossy and black.

My Almschi, Gustav wrote from Munich,
Why no letter yesterday? Are you hiding something?
At our parting, Walter promised secrecy.

But, *What's this?* Gustav asked, waving an envelope.
Here is a young fellow who asks for your hand.
From then on he clung to me, insisting

we sleep with the door between our bedrooms
flung open, demanding I carry in his meals.
I would find him weeping on the floor.

When Walter came to town I had no choice.
I told him no and put him on a train,
not without regrets. Home, I paused

in the doorway, blood heating my face,
to hear again my poor forgotten lieder.
These are good, Mahler declared from the piano.

*Dear God, was I blind? I won't rest
until you start working.* And years too late,
he played my old songs over again and again.

Mahler's Death

Once he'd pronounced my face
too smooth, too free from care.
When I am gone, he joked,
with your youth and looks

you will be in demand.
Whom shall you marry then?
I answered, *No one*,
thought I spoke the truth.

In Manhattan, he conducted
with an inflamed throat, mused
about his little streptococci,
how they slept and danced.

Aboard the ship his fever
dipped and swelled,
his lips burned, his eyes
darkened and shone. When we docked,

he bolted from the stretcher
to call a car, then paled
and dropped his head. *My life
has all been paper.* The journey

was a dying king's. Reporters
swarmed the train at every station.
Beneath the quilt, fingers conducting,
he spoke his last words: *Mozart! Mozart*!

In death he resembled
a candle. Slender and waxen,
still warm with the memory of flame.

Kokoschka

After our arguments—red and black
brushstrokes—he'd strew my bed
with rose petals. *Can't you paint
anything but Mummy?* Gucki would ask.
Against his will, my features
surfaced in each portrait. *Be my wife,*

in secret, while I am poor.
I was building a home on Semmering,
and in wet plaster Oskar slashed
my image pointing skyward, his
engulfed by serpents, both our bodies

torn by flame. Jealous of ghosts,
he thumbed through photographs
for Mahler's face, kissed each
silvery likeness, an act of white magic.
I was with child, and Oskar feared

his son might be born with Gustav's eyes.
When the box came—Mahler's death mask
packed in shavings—I knelt
to open it, and knew. In a clinic
I had the child taken. Kokoschka
sold his paintings, bought a mare,

enlisted, chiding me in endless letters:
*Don't write Corporal, only OK,
for that is who I am.* A bayonet
tore his lung, a bullet pierced
his skull, but still the letters came:

*My room is full of mortar,
dust and cold.* To slip away,
to buy some peace,
I married Walter Gropius.

Cut Flowers

Fallen nestling, all heartbeat, eyes,
and lofty forehead, Franz Werfel
sought me out. *If anyone alive*
can turn me into an artist,
he said, *it is you.*
Like barbed wire, my married name

lay across my skin, Walter's furloughs
so many months apart. In his family's
high-ceilinged rooms, I'd drop
my fork, spill wine on starched linen,
seeing myself as they must see me:
Social climber. Widow of a Jew.

A world crazed with color and noise
beckoned from beyond their windows.
Its emissary, Franz with his queer fervor
for revolution, his lazy love
of cafe life, whisky, cigarettes.
Franz who sent me poems like cut flowers—

vibrant and graceful, the stems
still weeping. Who got me with child
and in the seventh month made love to me
too hungrily. I awoke in blood,
sent Franz running for the doctor
through rain-soaked fields.

Of course I lived, to baptize my son,
to bury him, to tell
the necessary lies. Someone must live.

Alma at Eighty

Near the end, two rooms held all my life.
What rooms! Full as my life had been,
the uncracked spines of Werfel's books
coloring the shelves, my piano's
warm patina, and my portrait
rendered by Kokoschka, such heartless
golds and pinks some called him an assassin
of my face. This was New York,
the treetops swaying just outside,
the pearl gray light valuable
because it was so scarce.
Though geniuses grew fewer every year,
I kept champagne in stock for celebrations,
fresh flowers, deep chairs in a circle,
and though all my dresses were somber
I never skimped on pearls or pancake makeup,
and never once wore panties. *How impractical,*
restrictive, so much silk to weigh one down,
I'd say to shock the ingénues.
You're still a wild brat, Oskar wrote,
and so I tried to be. There were concerts
to attend as Mahler's widow, the audience
rising to applaud me, and brandy
—against doctor's orders—to lend my cheeks
some crimson. And to prove
great men still walked the earth,
a letter now and then from Thornton Wilder.
When I couldn't sleep, I'd remember:
crescendo dwindling to pianissimo;
large hands stained with pigment;
footsteps that shook the floor.

Last Words

It was given me to hold the reins
for the horsemen of light.

Now death,
I find, is handsome.
Death is the crown prince of Austria,
and he, too, desires me,
swears only I
must bear his children.
His whispered proposal is clumsy
but ardent, and

he needs me
to listen deeply, head tilted
at an angle suggesting
fascination, he needs
my hand in his larger hand,
bones cloaked in unassuming flesh,
muscles trained to never clench.

If there was a cost, I have forgotten.

Daylight

You're snarled in dreams, the complicated kind,
an epic cast of characters who flicker onscreen
to speak portentous words—*The onion!*
Always remember the onion!—promise to return
and don't. You blink awake.
Here's daylight, rationed by Venetian slats.
The stark outlines of rocking chair, shed clothes.
Your body, twin to the one you'd been feeding
through the projector, eager to dissolve
into the lightshow, black and white
and umpteen shades of silver. You bought the drama
wholesale, despite clues: a singing rosebush;
the absence of weather; gravity
and other rules suspended. Despite his touch
which should have tipped you off,
the faceless one who surfaces in dreams,
to still you, steel you, steal you,
calm hand on your shoulder blade,
to lead and levitate you through Auroras Borealis,
with a sense of purpose so convincing, who's to say
it isn't real? On your tongue, the dream taste
fades, no matter how you shut
your eyes, seek out your pillow's
coolest hollows, hard as you bargain away
these addled sheets, this disabusing sunshine,
all the straining throats of common birds.

What I Didn't Tell You

In postcards from Vienna, Genoa, Marseilles,
I told of dry bread and missed trains,
of how my pockets swelled with curdled sweets
that crumbled into dust on my tongue.
I tried to describe the local air,
how it bubbled in my lungs and buoyed me
out the hotel window after curfew,
down unlit streets to a strip
of bleached rock. How I stretched
on a boulder, thin nightgown flapping,
and imagined the sea's dark
muscular arms. All that summer I lived
on strange new food: the pollen
from narcotic trees, banjos and trumpets
of buskers, the jangle of pfennigs
in their hats, the white moth of a kiss
blown from a boy's plump lips
in the Florentine gigolo district.
These things I could explain but not
the heart of it: how I lay
with every man I met to feel the bones
of my face change shape in his hands.
How I stole what I chose
from each: this one's eyes, dark and wet
as coffee grounds, that one's burnt
sienna moustache, this one's milky way
of red freckles, that one's taste of schnapps
and powdered sugar. I became them all,
sleek, rangy and brave, cut my hair,
wore my shoulders bare, let the sun
burnish my skin till it grew polished

as copper and, when I walked, the muscles
in my legs twanged like guitar strings.
I was swift as a pickpocket,
schooled in the ways
of the swallow, who even in a flock
traces her own peculiar loops
against the sky.

Girl

Plug her in, she's yours, twenty-four/seven,
the girl who glows and beckons from your screen.
Unfurling like a one-armed bandit's jackpot,
her body parts skirl past, bathed in blue light,
as lush as plums or cherries or split melon.
The airy tits of one girl float like clouds
above another's mega-legs, an ass
spliced from yet a third, these random fragments
assembled into woman by your eye,
real as a model airplane. If she speaks,
her come-on lines are scripted. If she's wrapped,
she's easy to unwrap; between her skin
and your parched lips nothing but convex glass.
Smiling is her job. She knows you want her
because who wouldn't? Hell, I want her too
or want to be her, sometimes, in the buzz
after I've stared too long, my flesh exhausted
by its own weight, my skin's dull tendency
to slough off into dust, the daily tug
toward obsolescence. I would hone my legs down—
they're all wrong—inject my lips with honey,
and paint my smile white as the Parthenon.
Beauty is truth, truth beauty—that is all?

No, beauty is the lie we'd carve and starve for.
We'd suck it till the juice ran down our arms,
or live inside it like a suit of armor—
if only that were possible. Instead
we lie here, shipwrecked by her ceaseless motion.
Reaching for her prow, we catch her wake.

On Leafing Through a Catalogue
of William Bailey's Paintings

His women, cool and grave.
His still lifes, women.
The vase, its slender neck
melting into sloped shoulders.
The spread mouths of bowls.
And eggs, white or tan,
each poised at the center
of its own liquid shadow.

The light's clinical, the table set
less for a feast than a dissection.
The walls are brown as tea leaves
left to boil. These rooms
aren't rooms, but if they were,
the windows would be curtainless,
cracked open. The smell would be
electrical, an overheated spot.

Turn the page, and S. sits waiting
with a gaze that says
she knew we were bringing
our rough fingertips and greedy eyes.
The painter knows us too, knows how
to make us look: her dress rolled down
past comfort, the nipples
that mirror her blank brown eyes.

Once he's got us, he makes us see
deeper than we'd choose.
Hands clasped, arms trapped by fabric,
she's a pattern of shadows and luster,
a cluster of eggs displayed on a table,
a long, fallopian throat.

Portrait in Negative Space

A child places a paper doll
on cardboard and crayons furiously
over the figure, then lifts
to find the cool white shape of woman
cut from an orange flame burst, the nimbus
brighter for its missing core.
That's how I picture the absence
of the woman you refused—
a void an x-ray could detect,
black as a knot in your white aorta.
In person, she was beautiful enough,
but her elbows were rough, her laugh
a sort of bleat. Gone, she's something else.
A complicated shape time erodes
to cookie cutter neatness—
flip of hair, triangle of skirt—
till you can find no real woman's image
smooth enough to plug the hole she left.
Wherever she may be, she's less present
than here, where she isn't, her notness
a bubble that moves to part your blood,
her memory the small craft
your *no* set in motion.

Erotomania

1. Diane G.

The way an onion's scent
clings to my fingers, refuses
to be camouflaged

by hand cream or perfume. The way
that same onion, eaten,
floats through the body's pores
so the skin exhales it, and I walk

in its brassy aura. This is how
you first invaded me, how I carry you
inside me, release you

into the world. At my hip,
a quarter and two pennies
still warm from your hand.
In my arms, the bag you packed,

bulky as an infant. Red peppers,
nectarines. One silken avocado.
In my kitchen I pare the dark rind,

slip slice after slice down my throat,
so my dreams will be full
of flesh smooth as cream, green as willows.
Forbidden to speak, we've found a language

more vivid than words: bleeding strawberries,
the dull ache of mushrooms, winter squash
with its heart of sticky seed, and garlic,

each lone clove potent as a bullet.
My days would blur to gray, would smell
of damp newspaper and bottled cologne,
without the light dance of your fingertips

across my palm, the shared, off-kilter smile,
without the fragrant weight of cantaloupe,
grapes tinged with frost, parsley like bundled lace.

2. Margaret N.

The *scree* of shopkeepers tugging up
their iron gates. Footsteps on pavement.
The slightly sour warmth of baking bread
rising into my half-sleep like a promise.

Then the abrupt and daily remembering

how I said a wrong word,
and you hardened yourself against me,
your voice on the phone like setting cement
and after so many months of saying
there was nothing I could say
so you would hear. How would it be

to know the fingers
that paint my sleeping skin with flame
can't be real, to know your dreaming hands
can't be finding their way into mine.

How must it be to trust
what's actual is best?

This overcast sky, coffee
roasting in the shop downstairs,
and on my balcony
doves that mumble
and purr over crumbs.

3.

The clinically delusional don't ask
what am I getting into
is this reciprocal
am I worth loving
what if I change my mind?

Like saints, they swoon,
pierced through by lightning.
Roses bloom on their spread palms.

The rest of us ask questions
till we scare ourselves silly.
No news here: to love, we must go
a little mad. How else to relax

till our skin blurs and softens
and the world seeps in?
Till the blue, diffuse light
we struggle to contain
bursts from our pores, a nimbus?

4. David R.

Sprinkled in this envelope, please find
twenty-three eyelashes, the body part
most like my devotion—
rooted in flesh, invisible
to the careless eye. You'll know
to conceal this offering at bedtime
under your spun sugar hair.
Pressed to your ear,
my lashes will rustle in code
how you swim through my nights,
naked as a seal. How in daylight

your shadow eludes me, white on the sidewalk
where others fall dark. How I walk
sixteen paces back to catch your reflection
stuttering from window to window
while you pretend indifference,
your staccato steps,
the exact tilt of your chin
mine to decipher.
You wonder: *Would I die for you?*
Would I kill? I wonder:
Does the skin beneath your nightgown
shimmer aquarium blue?
Everything about you shines: your teeth,
the whites of your eyes. Your tongue.
Like the square of light your window casts,
molten patch of grass
where I hunker and wait.

5. Elizabeth M.

I open my throat, say *aaah*
and his flashlight warms my tongue.
His fingers probe the hollows
behind my earlobes, the glands
at the base of my neck.

When he listens to me, he shuts his eyes—
black-lashed, sloe-brown, well-deep.
With a stethoscope, he laps my skin.
My heartbeats squeeze through the cord,
sprint uphill, leap into his ears.

For his touch, I slog through puddles,
coat unzipped to sleet. I touch doorknobs,

seek out crowds. Sometimes at night,
I simply say out loud: *my throat hurts.*
By morning, the red carpet's unfurled.

He gives me words I can't decipher,
paper I trade for a potion
I'll hold on my tongue
like communion wine. I shouldn't say this.
Once a year, I spread myself

inside out, receive the speculum's sharp tongue,
for a chance to watch his rapt face,
to feel his gloved and gentle fingers
prodding and swabbing, prizing me
down to my very cells. And when I moan,

I see his face go tender.
I'm hurting you? he asks,
and *No*, I lie. *You're not.*

6.

This voice is mine, the one behind the hands
typing this confession. Once you know
you'll diagnose me crazy, like those others.
Once there was a man. Well, there were several
who all were him, his narrow hands, his sharp
cheekbones, his way of drawing lines: *We're sane.*
Just the two of us. The rest are fucked.
I starved for his approval, studied hard
to pass his oblique tests: Did I like curry?
The Rolling Stones? Show tunes? *Citizen Kane?*
I'd try to guess the answer that would please
my boyfriend; I erased myself to draw
a fake, perfected self the way a starlet
shaves her brows to pencil new ones in.
I saw how he despised me for my backflips,

but couldn't stop. *You shouldn't dye your hair*
just because I'm hot for blondes, he said.
I shouldn't, but I did. The man I married
is someone else. I can say anything
obtuse, belch on the street, wear ragged sweats.
What's sick: freed of the lion tamer's whip,
his absentminded pats, sometimes
I'm homesick for the feel of sailing through,
my hair unsinged. I miss those burning hoops.

First Kiss

This collision of teeth, of tongues and lips,
is like feeling for the door
in a strange room, blindfolded.
He imagines he knows her
after four dates, both of them taking pains
to laugh correctly, to make eye contact.
She thinks at least this long first kiss
postpones the moment she'll have to face
four white walls, the kitchen table,
its bowl of dried petals and nutmeg husks,
the jaunty yellow vase with one jaunty bloom,
the answering machine's one bloodshot eye.

Kokoschka's Doll

Raw-boned and klutzy, with an archangel's
blue gaze, Oskar Kokoschka slashed his canvases
with layers of paint, juicy and glistening,
in the Vienna of *Schlagsahne* and gaslit cafes,
the Great War edging in at the margins,
every doorway lush with the flourishes
of art nouveau. Kokoschka painted himself
shimmering in wistful stasis, legs pressed
to the thighs of his lover, Alma Mahler.
The air that whirls about them is splintered
with impending loss, but for one spring green
glissando of a moment, he's got Alma
caged in his arm's pink crook.

But here under their framed gaze
in the beige living room, we hug our distinct
sides of the sofa, east against west.
For weeks, it seems, we've been like this,
stony as the lions on library steps.
But some nights, from our subterranean
burrows of sleep, something surfaces. Hands
I recognize as yours explore my rib cage,
the soft palms and work-scuffed fingers
crawling through my dreams with a stern
determination that startles me awake.
Sometimes desire runs amuck, the man-made dam
compelling a river into many crooked streams.
So it happened when Oskar came back

from the front, wounded and addled,
and found his love had sidled offstage
with a famous architect. In the sanitorium,

he turned to art and commissioned a doll,
life sized, in Alma's shape.
For months he peppered the seamstress with letters:
Give special care to the dimensions
of the head, the ribcage, the rump and limbs.
And take to heart the belly's curve.
Can the mouth open? Are there teeth
and a tongue inside? While he waited,
he bought the doll a trousseau
and wrote more letters: *Does no one know*
about the doll? I would die of jealousy
if some man were allowed to see
or touch her nakedness. Some evenings

on the bus ride home, from behind my spread
newspaper, I'll appraise the faces
of strangers backlit by streaming landscape.
And the angles that attract me most
are like yours: the taut cheekbones, the dark
coppery eyes. One reckless time
I jumped off the bus to follow a man
with your profile. I trailed him
four blocks east, three north,
turned back and rode home to refuse
your welcoming kiss, retreated to the couch,
my edge of it, to fume over what makes dreams
simpler to embrace than life. Oskar's doll

had to be a disappointment, its "lifelike skin"
a sheath of coarse fur stitched
at its neck and soles. Even the face
was no less and no more than a mask.
Still, he propped it in his carriage,
drove it to restaurants, demanded
a place be set. And he hired

a maid to dress his doll, to curl its wig,
to lift silver spoonfuls of hot food
to its lips, and she, the maid,
a country girl, fresh faced and canny,
took pity one night, led Oskar
to the cellar and slipped from her clothes.
But the history of happiness shifts.
Soon she was carving his initials—*O.K.*
—into her breast with a knife.

Aversive Therapy

When I knew, finally knew, I had to stop
loving you, but wasn't sure I could
since all it took to melt me was my nickname
murmured in your voice, your long-lashed eyes,
impressions of your skin pressed hard to mine,
I tried aversive therapy. At bedtime
I'd conjure up your cheekbones, their sharp marble,
skin fine as sand, shoulder blades crisp as wings,
while dragging onstage memories of the summer
you banged bones with a lifeguard while I waited
for a phone call, a postcard. Next the night
I found her letters and was sick enough
to read them all. These memories sufficed
to scorch my throat with bile, to spur my pulse,
and there were random lies and callous words,
to couple with the gold thread of your legs,
your damp, abundant curls, your narrow hands,
until your very name took on the gutterals
of a Sicilian curse, your grinning portrait
became a skull and crossbones. Thus I banished you
but also—though I didn't see till now—
I sent away the girl who leaned against you
in snapshots, the brown girl on her red bicycle,
her hair blown back by wind off the Atlantic
(same cool blue as your eyes) her smile as simple,
as milk white, as the moth that bumps a lamp
and bumps again, again, stunned, and again,
that girl who knew exactly what she loved.

Learning to Float

Relax. It's like love. Keep your lips
moist and parted, let your upturned hands
unfold like water lilies, palms exposed.

Breathe deeply, slowly. Forget chlorine
and how the cement bottom was stained
blue so the water looks clear

and Caribbean. Ignore the drowned mosquitoes,
the twigs that gather in the net
of your hair. The sun is your ticket,

your narcotic, blessing your chin,
the floating islands of your knees.
Shut your eyes and give yourself

to the pulsating starfish, purple and red,
that flicker on your inner lids.
Hallucination is part of the process,

like amnesia. Forget how you learned
to swim, forget being told
Don't panic. Don't worry. Let go

of my neck. It's only water. Don't think
unless you're picturing Chagall,
his watercolors of doves and rooftops,

lovers weightless as tissue,
gravity banished, the dissolving voices
of violins and panpipes. The man's hand

circles the woman's wrist so loosely,
what moors her permits her to float,
and she rises past the water's skin,

above verandas and the tossing heads
of willows. Her one link to earth,
his light—almost reluctant—touch, is a rope

unfurling, slipping her past the horizon,
into the cloud-stirring current. This far up,
what can she do but trust he won't let go?

Beard

The bristles sprout swiftly,
in a single direction like pines
leaning into wind. When you sleep
I notice each hair
wears its own peculiar shade,
as many browns as there are names of trees:
chestnut, ash, redwood, silver beech.
Each rankles against my cheek,
casts its own blue shadow.
At your chest, a coarse black tangle
thins to a ridge, leads me
down to that red protective nest
of found hay and barbered corkscrew curls.
You toss and tug the blanket
to your ears, exposing
bony feet, the ankles
tapered and graceful,
calves thick as larches
softened by moss. When I say
I know you, what is it
I know? This sinuous path
from chin to soles? I thought I knew
your face—crisp lashes,
cheek muscles twitching
with the speech of dreams—
but this beard you've chosen to grow
eclipses half. The more I stare,
the more your edges blur,
and your name on my tongue
dissolves to babble,
takes other words with it:
husband, lover, brother, father, stranger.

Crystal

It began as accident, a moment
beside you on a bench, our forearms touching.
(You didn't pull away; neither did I.)
As if our skins were porous and your soul
were liquid, you poured into me.
                                        Like crystal,
my voice took on a new note, full of you,
and from your voice I knew you likewise full,
our conversation vibrant as the chime
of champagne glasses touched in celebration,
a fragile music tuned by borrowed contents,
each narrow flute enriched by what it holds
the song provisional, the precise note
inspiring thirst, but altered by a sip.

The Rubin Vase

Suppose I say the hardest thing to say.
In a famous drawing two black silhouettes
gaze at each other, noses almost touching.
The viewer looks away, then glances back
and sees a different picture, a white chalice,
blank space between the faces seeping forward
to claim her eye. It's the profiles or the cup,
never both at once. The space between
two people—between us—can ebb or surge,
insistent as high tide seizing the shore.
Your fingers graze my chin, your body lowers
to press against my upward-arching body.
What I feel is that thin film of air
between our skins. These are the words that lurk
between the words I say. One day I can't
abide your touch; the next day I can't stand
its absence. Though the inner eye can't hold
two views at once, there's still the nagging sense
that with a blink the picture could change back.
Why should I say what echoes in my silence,
as if you've never seen the chasm between us,
as if, once seen, it could be overlooked.

Further Reading

I urge readers who enjoyed the poems on the life of Alma Mahler Werfel to seek out the following works, which provided my initial inspiration:

Keegan, Susanne. *The Bride of the Wind: The Life and Times of Alma Mahler-Werfel*. New York: Viking Penguin, 1983.

La Grange, Henry-Louis de. *Mahler*, vol. 1. Garden City, New York: Doubleday & Company, 1973.

Mahler-Werfel, Alma with E. B. Ashton. *And the Bridge is Love*. New York: Harcourt & Brace, 1958.

———. *The Diaries, 1898-1902*. Translated by Anthony Beaumont. Ithaca: Cornell University Press, 1999.

Monson, Karen. *Alma Mahler, Muse to Genius*. Boston: Houghton Mifflin Company, 1983.

Whitford, Frank. *Oskar Kokoschka, A Life*. New York: Athaneum, 1986.

Selected by Robert Fink, *Skin* is the eleventh winner of the Walt McDonald First-Book Competition in Poetry. The Competition is supported generously through donated subscriptions from *The American Scholar, The Atlantic Monthly, The Georgia Review, Gulf Coast, The Hudson Review, The Massachusetts Review, Poetry, Shenandoah,* and *The Southern Review.*